TWELVE STEPS TO SELF-IMPROVEMENT

A Crisp Assessment Profile

A FIFTY-MINUTE™ SERIES BOOK

CRISP PUBLICATIONS, INC.
Menlo Park, California

TWELVE STEPS TO SELF-IMPROVEMENT
A Crisp Assessment Profile

CREDITS
Editor: **Michael Crisp**
Layout and Composition: **Interface Studio**
Cover Design: **Carol Harris**
Artwork: **Ralph Mapson**

English language Crisp books are distributed worldwide. Our major international distributors include:

CANADA: Reid Publishing Ltd., Box 69559—109 Thomas St., Oakville, Ontario, Canada L6J 7R4. TEL: (905) 842-4428, FAX: (905) 842-9327

Raincoast Books Distribution Ltd., 112 East 3rd Avenue, Vancouver, British Columbia, Canada V5T 1C8. TEL: (604) 873-6581, FAX: (604) 874-2711

AUSTRALIA: Career Builders, P.O. Box 1051, Springwood, Brisbane, Queensland, Australia 4127. TEL: 841-1061, FAX: 841-1580

NEW ZEALAND: Career Builders, P.O. Box 571, Manurewa, Auckland, New Zealand. TEL: 266-5276, FAX: 266-4152

JAPAN: Phoenix Associates Co., Mizuho Bldg. 2-12-2, Kami Osaki, Shinagawa-Ku, Tokyo 141, Japan. TEL: 3-443-7231, FAX: 3-443-7640

Selected Crisp titles are also available in other languages. Contact International Rights Manager Suzanne Kelly at (415) 323-6100 for more information.

Library of Congress Catalog Card Number 90-85867
The Editors, Crisp Publications, Inc.
Twelve Steps to Self-Improvement
ISBN 1-56052-102-3

This book is printed on recyclable paper with soy ink.

INTRODUCTION

When times get tough, it is easy for a person to lose his or her enthusiasm and turn negative. Such down periods are accelerated when organizations are forced by external conditions such as domestic and international competition and/or a recession to tighten their belts. During these times, the survivors will need to get greater productivity from employees.

The British have an expression ''I'm going on holiday to sort things out.'' All of us occasionally feel the need to get away and gain a new focus on our careers or our lives in general. Some of us take a short vacation to go through the process. Others can do it over a weekend at home. Still others ''sort things out'' by taking a long drive in the country.

During these restoration periods, it is a good idea to view yourself as a battery that has started to lose its energy and needs a recharge. Consider the ''recharge machine'' to be this book. The self-improvement inventory (profile) you will be taking will measure how well you have charged your battery.

One other thought.

Why not forget the conditions that existed in the past and accept more demanding challenges that can also lead to success in the future?

It is the smart thing to do!

Good luck!

Michael G. Crisp

PUBLISHER

> "*When the going gets tough, the tough get going.*"
>
> **Cher**
> **(among others)**

CONTENTS

(continued, overleaf)

P A R T

I

Rating Yourself In Twelve Categories

Category 1

How High Is Your Self-Esteem?

·CAN DO·

WHAT IS SELF-ESTEEM?

Self-esteem is the way you perceive yourself. If you view yourself as inferior to others, or as having little confidence to do everyday things, you are lacking in self-esteem. If, on the other hand, you are full of confidence and consider yourself to be competent in most situations, you have good self-esteem. Those perceived as having high self-esteem are often chosen as leaders when presented with an opportunity.

Self-esteem translates into self-worth. When you place a high value on yourself as a person, you respect your skills and abilities and have confidence in what you can accomplish. If you have self-esteem, you do not back away from challenges. You are a professional!

Education can help give people self-esteem. For example, those who have attended college often exhibit more self-worth than do those without. *But not always.* Many non-college educated people, through experience and self-improvement demonstrate a greater degree of self-esteem than those with degrees.

Having a high degree of self-esteem usually gives one a comfortable, secure feeling inside that manifests itself in a positive, confident attitude. This is good news, but people who think well of themselves still need to be sensitive when building relationships with others.

Self-esteem is a precious commodity that needs to be balanced with a degree of humility.

HOW HIGH IS YOUR SELF-ESTEEM?*

> **INSTRUCTIONS:**
> Mark a ''T'' for true or ''F'' for false after each statement as it normally relates to your thinking.

_____ 1. I feel my work/career has progressed more because of luck and not because I deserve it.

_____ 2. I often find myself thinking, ''Why can't I be more successful?''

_____ 3. I do not believe I am working up to my potential.

_____ 4. I consider it a failure when I do not accomplish my goals.

_____ 5. When others are nice to me I often feel suspicious.

_____ 6. Giving others compliments about their strengths often makes me feel uncomfortable.

_____ 7. It is difficult to see co-workers promoted because I often feel I am more deserving.

_____ 8. I do not necessarily believe that my mind has a direct influence on my physical well being.

_____ 9. When things are going well, they usually will not last for me.

_____ 10. I place a high value on what others think of me.

_____ 11. I like to impress my supervisor.

_____ 12. I find it difficult to face up to my mistakes.

_____ 13. I am not comfortable always saying what I mean.

*This exercise is taken from the book _Developing Self Esteem_ by Connie Palladino, Ph.D.

_____ 14. I find it hard to say I am sorry.

_____ 15. I tend to accept change in my job slowly because of fear.

_____ 16. Procrastination is a good word to describe my work habits.

_____ 17. I often find myself thinking, "Why even try, I won't make it."

_____ 18. When my boss praises me, I usually do not believe him or her.

_____ 19. I do not think my co-workers want me to advance professionally.

_____ 20. I avoid people who I think do not like me.

_____ 21. My attitude toward life could improve.

_____ 22. If honest with myself, I tend to blame my parents for how my life is turning out.

_____ 23. I find it difficult to look for the good in others.

_____ 24. I do not think people can change their attitudes.

_____ 25. I really do not believe that a self-help book will make a difference in my self-esteem.

Add up all your TRUE and FALSE statements.

TRUE: _____ **FALSE:** _____

If you scored over half of the items "TRUE," you may want to spend some quality time with yourself, or with a counselor, thinking about your life. Think about why you have these feelings.

If the majority of your answers were "FALSE" you seem to have good self-esteem and are on your way to greater success and satisfaction.

On the following page you will find two cases. Study them carefully and then compare your thoughts with those of the authors.

CASE STUDIES

CASE NUMBER 1

Jill always seems to be down on her abilities and appearance. For some reason she does not look as good to herself as she does to others. If Jill were to rate her self-image on a scale of one to ten, her rating would be three or four.

Her low rating is partially due to the fact that Jill honestly believes her parents did not expect her to achieve as much as her older sister who was always a good student and school leader. Another reason is because Jill seldom sticks up for herself at work or during family situations. Rather than communicate her true feelings, she usually just walks away.

Jill, in her first job since leaving school, is underemployed based on her abilities and skills. If her self-esteem had been higher, management would have provided several promotional opportunities in the past three years.

If you had a close relationship with Jill how would you assist her to go about building her self-esteem to a higher level?

CASE NUMBER 2

James is a highly respected and competent employee. He is a consistently high producer, seldom absent, and works well with fellow employees. James frequently works overtime because co-workers lean on him for help during regular office hours. He is conservative in his grooming.

James hopes to eventually become a manager, but he refuses to see himself as a leader. Although others might consider him to be a "soft touch," he can, at times, take a firm stand on an important matter. A university graduate, James is currently taking night courses in preparation for an MBA.

On a scale of one to ten, James would rate himself about a five as far as self-esteem is concerned. He recognizes that he needs to communicate a more positive and assertive image; but, so far, he is content to remain as a likable member of his work group. Social acceptance is more important at this stage than a big career-step upward.

What suggestions would you make to James if he came to you for help in improving his self-esteem?

To compare your thoughts with those of the author please turn to page 103.

SELF-INVENTORY SCALE

It is now time for you to rate yourself on a specific scale. This scale will be used for all twelve categories covered in this book. Please follow the instructions below carefully.

On a scale of 1 to 10, rate your honest perception in the area of your SELF-ESTEEM. Do this by circling the appropriate number on the scale below.

- If you circle the number 1, 2, or 3, you are saying you need *significant* improvement to reach your potential.

- If you circle the number 4, 5, or 6 you are recording that you need *considerable* improvement to reach your potential.

- Should you circle an 8, 9, or 10 you are asserting that you need *little* or *no* improvement to reach your potential.

Please be honest with yourself. Keep in mind the middle of the scale is average. Most people rate themselves somewhere in the middle of the scale. Take your time. It will be from ratings similar to this that you will build your individual profile on page 92 of the book.

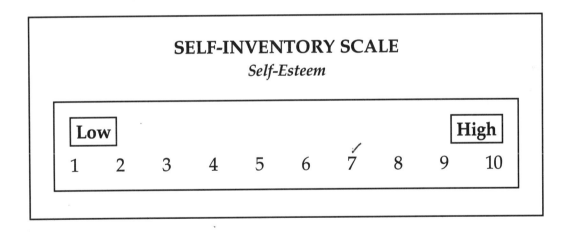

Category 2

Do You See The Wellness-Success Connection?

WELLNESS DEFINED

The intriguing thing about wellness is that you tend to know when you enjoy it and when you don't. When you are well, there is normally a feeling of vitality and personal confidence. You feel in tune with your environment. Your energy is high. When unwell, you feel tired, draggy, and down. Nothing seems right.

The diagram shown above illustrates three major contributing factors to wellness.

PHYSICAL EXERCISE. Those who are involved in physical fitness know the benefits it brings. Regular exercisers understand that a person not only feels better following a workout but he or she is building a stronger body for the future.

PROPER DIET. Good nutrition is essential. In addition to giving your body the necessary vitamins and minerals, a proper diet helps ''normalize'' weight. Coordinating an exercise program with a proper diet is the best of both worlds. It takes time, effort, and sometimes help from an outside source to achieve consistent results.

MENTAL HEALTH. Although exercise and diet may be the primary sources of wellness, both need to be viewed from the perspective of mental health. Each supports the other, and it is the combination of all three that adds up to true wellness.

Wellness, then, is a holistic concept, saying that the sum (wellness) can be greater than all the contributing parts. When you weave all three elements into one fabric you have the foundation upon which to build your professional career. Without wellness your personal goals and dreams may never be achieved.

WELLNESS AND THE ATTITUDE CONNECTION

Apparently no one has been able to prove conclusively a clinical relationship between physical well-being and attitude. Most, however, including the most cynical of researchers in the area, concede there is a connection. Please answer the following questions and compare your answers with those of the author.

True False

☐ ☐ 1. Exercise can do more to adjust your attitude than a cocktail "happy hour."

☐ ☐ 2. Following a good diet has nothing to do with improving your self-image.

☐ ☐ 3. The better you feel physically on a given day, the more positive your attitude is apt to be.

☐ ☐ 4. Neither a sense of physical well-being nor a positive attitude can be stored indefinitely.

☐ ☐ 5. Daily exercise can do little to keep one positive.

AUTHOR'S ANSWERS: 1. T (both will change your focus, but exercise is better for you and lasts longer; 2. F; 3. T; 4. T; 5. F (Daily exercise is an outstanding attitude adjuster).

TYPICAL WELLNESS COMMENTS

More than any previous time in our history, our nation is aware of physical fitness. A surprising number of us incorporate daily workouts into our schedules. This commitment to the ''attitude connection'' is expressed in these typical comments.

> ''My workout does as much for my mental state as it does for my body.''

> ''Exercise tones up my body and tunes up my outlook.''

> ''I never underestimate what my daily workout does for me psychologically.''

Many fitness enthusiasts depend upon exercise to keep them out of attitudinal ruts.

> ''I've renamed my health club The Attitude Adjustment Factory.''

> ''When I'm worried or depressed, I take a long walk. It has a way of pushing negative thoughts out of my system.''

> ''A tough workout can get me out of a mental rut.''

No single group in our society deals more with the psychological aspects of attitude than professional athletes. Increasingly, athletes engage year-round in sophisticated physical conditioning programs. They realize they must stay in shape to remain competitive. If you listen carefully, coaches and managers talk more about attitude than physical conditioning.

> ''We made the playoffs this year because we have a new team attitude.''

> ''I owe my success this season to my coach. He helped me adjust not only my technique, but more importantly my attitude.''

> ''My success this year is because of greater self-confidence. I finally began to believe in myself.''

As important as talent and physical conditioning are, most players, coaches, and sportscasters talk about mental attitude as most important.

They must be trying to tell us something.

CASE STUDIES

CASE NUMBER 3

Genelle is your favorite co-worker. She has become a good friend. Genelle is efficient, effective, and builds excellent relationships both on the job and in her personal world, but she has an image problem due primarily to her excessive weight.

Genelle is always on a new weight-loss program. When the program is successful and she loses some weight, she becomes upbeat, productive, and creative. But she always seems to abandon the program after awhile and regains the weight. When this happens, she becomes slightly negative and withdrawn and falls into a productivity slump.

Genelle knows the up-and-down pattern she follows and has come to you for guidance. What suggestions would you make?

CASE NUMBER 4

Maggie is concerned about her husband for two reasons. First, whatever activity Karl goes into (running, cycling, windsurfing) he overdoes it and, as a result, suffers excessive exhaustion. Sometimes it takes him two or three days to get his full energy level back. Second, although it happens infrequently, he is so competitive that when he does well in an event he celebrates too much with his many friends and this further breaks down his energy level.

Maggie does not feel that Karl understands the true meaning of wellness, and she fears he is damanging his long-term health. She has used the term ''moderation'' so often that using it further is meaningless.

How might Maggie protect Karl from his own excesses?

Turn to page 103 for the views of the author.

SELF-INVENTORY SCALE

It is now time for you to rate yourself on your state of wellness as it has existed during the past year. As you do this, consider the following factors:

- The kind of exercise regimen you have consistently practiced.
- The nutrition program you have followed throughout the year.
- Your use of tobacco, alcohol, and drugs.
- Weight maintenance at the level you desire.
- The success you have had in managing stress.
- Your ability to relax and sleep normal hours.
- How well you have been able to "balance your life."

Do not give yourself a high rating unless you have earned it.

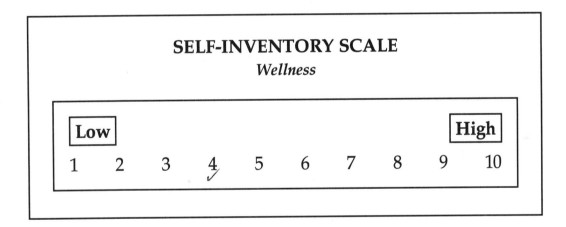

Category 3

Are You A Good Communicator?

THE ART OF COMMUNICATION

Hundreds of excellent books have been written about aspects of communication. Some publications place emphasis on interpersonal communication, others deal primarily with group communication dynamics, still others concentrate on organizational communication. A few specialize on platform or public speaking.

Obviously, it is difficult to be a star communicator. For most employees, good communication is mainly devoted to *keeping people well informed*. This means co-workers, superiors, family, and friends. Not an easy assignment!

People rated high as communicators are not reluctant to speak up. They can verbalize their feelings. Good communicators do not hide important information from others; they quickly correct misunderstandings through communications, and perhaps most important of all, they *listen*. Good communicators recognize that others need to know enough so that they feel like a part of things. Good communicators accept the premise that communication is the life blood of relationships. In short, if you want to really get along with people, you need to be able to effectively communicate with them.

As a general rule, the following is true:

- Quiet, introspective, introverted people often stay in their shells and undercommunicate. Thus, although they may have a great deal to contribute, they are often misinterpreted.

- Highly verbal, assertive, extroverted people often talk too much and too forcefully. Thus, they run the risk of offending others.

A good communicator is able to keep people informed in a sensitive manner without damaging relationships. Turn the page and learn why good communicators are also good listeners.

THE BEST COMMUNICATORS ARE GOOD LISTENERS

As you evaluate yourself as a communicator take into consideration your ability as a listener. Most of us listen at only 25% of our ability. How would your closest friends rate you? Your boss? Your family? Would some people suggest that you should talk less and listen more?

Listed below are some suggestions that can improve your listening skills. Check those that are applicable to you. I know how to:

☐ Send people signals through my eyes and body gestures so that they know I am listening.

☐ Relax when communicating to others so they will feel comfortable about adding their comments.

☐ Slow my mind down when listening so that I won't anticipate what people say before they say it.

☐ Improve my concentration.*

☐ Avoid forming a reply before I hear the other person out.

☐ Not be defensive about my point of view during communication.

☐ Keep my voice soft rather than loud and aggressive.

CASE STUDIES

CASE NUMBER 5

About three years ago Charlie was deeply hurt and disturbed by something a superior said to him. Since then, communication with that person has been infrequent and emotionally charged. Looking back, Charlie can now see that this lack of communication has damaged his career and turned him negative on corporate life in general.

How much of the fault is Charlie's?

CASE NUMBER 6

Melissa, known in her hospital ward as the "quiet nurse," was influenced by her family and Hispanic culture to be submissive and communicate only on special occasions. Although she did well in college and is recognized as a highly-skilled registered nurse, she speaks more with patients than co-workers.

In some respects Melissa is an ideal nurse. She folows the rules, is always on time, never complains, and adheres to suggestions of others even though she does not offer many herself. The only problem is that Melissa is misinterpreted by others because she doesn't communicate. A few think she feels she is too good for her job. Others feel she doesn't like her peers. The supervisor rates her outstanding as an isolated employee but poor as a team member.

If you were Melissa's supervisor, what suggestions would you make in a counseling situation?

Turn to page 103 for the author's views.

RATING YOURSELF AS A COMMUNICATOR

So far you have rated yourself on self-esteem and wellness. Now it is time to rate yourself as a communicator. This may be your most difficult evaluation. Please take your time and ask yourself the following questions before you circle what you honestly believe is the most accurate number on the scale.

- Do people listen to you?
- Do you receive compliments on your speaking or listening?
- Do you hold back too much when you know you have something important to say?
- Do you initiate conversations?
- Do you feel comfortable in speaking to your supervisor on sensitive subjects?
- Do you consider yourself an expert in communicating over the telephone?
- Do you over-talk?
- Do you speak too loudly? Too softly?

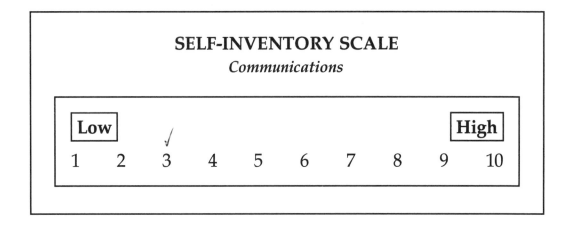

SELF-INVENTORY SCALE
Communications

Low									High
1	2	3 ✓	4	5	6	7	8	9	10

Category 4

How Good Are You At Human Relations?

STAYING POSITIVE IN A NEGATIVE ENVIRONMENT

How positive or negative is your workplace? Do some co-workers have a personality conflict with the boss? Do some employees purposefully avoid others? Is there a negative clique of workers who constantly complain and make it more difficult for others?

Some work environments are measurably more positive than others. How positive or negative individual work environments are is often due to the manager in charge. Sometimes morale is due to a combination of factors hard to pinpoint and harder to control. The fact is, the number one reason for job unhappiness and low productivity, centers around relationship conflicts, which in most cases, could have been avoided.

Working in a negative environment and keeping yourself positive is not an easy game to play. Yet, at one time or another, everyone must deal with the problem. Regardless of your situation, if you are to reach your career goals, your three major human relations challenges are:

- Learning to work with negative people without becoming negative yourself.

- Keeping relationships as healthy as possible—especially with your supervisor.

- Repairing damaged relationships as soon as possible.

The primary reasons why success in these areas will boost your career are:

- Good human relations will improve your personal productivity as well as help others cooperate to get the job done.

- Your image within the company will be more positive.

- The reduction of personal conflicts will take less out of you and, as a result, make you a more valuable employee.

TIPS ON HOW TO STAY POSITIVE

 TIP #1: Value your own positive attitude to the point where you refuse to let others tarnish it. Keep reminding yourself that your attitude is your most priceless possession, and it belongs to *you*—not your organization or your family.

 TIP #2: Be pleasant and communicate with negative co-workers. Encourage them to be more positive by being a good model—but avoid spending too much off-work time (lunch and coffee breaks) with them. Do whatever it takes to keep your personal productivity up even though those who are negative may not.

 TIP #3: Get suggestions from your supervisor on the kind of role he or she wants you to play so that you help keep departmental morale high. Ask if you are setting a good example. Is it helping? What else can you do? It is good for the supervisor to know you want to contribute to team productivity.

To stay positive when those around you are negative is a difficult challenge, but letting others pull you into their negative way of thinking is a price too high to pay. Those who find the challenge too demanding often move to a new environment and start over.

REPAIRING RELATIONSHIPS

If good communication is the life blood of any healthy relationship, then a transfusion of free, open communication should be the first order of business in any relationship repair. It is important to select the right time (when you think the other party will be receptive), the right place (private and free from interruptions), and the discussion should open in a quiet, non-threatening manner.

Once the time and place are "right" and both parties are comfortable, you should state in your own way that you would like to discuss a "win-win" system that will restore the relationship and keep it healthy. You should invite the other party to describe what it will take to adjust the system so that both parties will benefit in the future.

> It took Jeanne three days to gather up her nerve and select the right time to open a discussion with Harry over their recent "falling out." Although she was awkward in getting the conversation going and introducing her interpretation of a "win-win" theory, Harry picked up on the idea and within twenty minutes they had constructed a new reward system that formed the basis of a new and better working relationship.

In most one-on-one human situations, some compromise is necessary if the relationship is to be maintained. Often a little "give" from one end will do the trick. More often, both parties must "soften" their position from time to time.

Why is compromise often so difficult?

One reason may be because many people establish such rigid and defiant positions to begin with that any compromise could be interpreted as "weakness" or "failure."

> Grenville took such a firm stand with his boss about not accepting a temporary assignment that he could not make himself compromise. Later, he discovered his stand had caused a serious conflict and he had second thoughts about compromising but it was too late.

SOMETIMES COMPROMISE IS NECESSARY

CASE STUDY

CASE NUMBER 7

Despite the fact Courtney knows she cannot easily duplicate her salary or benefits with a competitor, she has decided to give her supervisor two weeks notice this Friday. Her decision is based upon protecting her mental health. The working climate she must endure has become so negative she is in a continual state of depression.

Courtney knows that the company has provided good physical working conditions. No complaint there! It is simply the negative attitudes of three co-workers that are part of her team. These three individuals (all with seniority over Courtney) are so bitter about life that she becomes irritated and negative herself. Even the efforts of the supervisor who is aware of the problem have been to no avail.

Is Courtney making a good decision?

To compare your answer with that of the author, turn to page 104.

APPRAISING YOUR HUMAN RELATIONS SKILLS

As we have seen, some people are measurably better at protecting themselves from the negative attitudes of others. These lucky individuals seem able to throw up a protective shield and stay positive no matter what. These same people are often good at creating positive relationships and repairing them when things turn sour. We can call these workers *human relations smart!*

How good are you in protecting your positive attitude and working well with others? As you rate yourself on the scale below, please take the following into consideration.

- The value you place on your positive attitude.

- The importance you place on good human relations.

- Your tolerance level regarding the behavior of others.

- Your freedom from prejudice.

- Your sensitivity to the relationship between good human relations and productivity.

If you have the reputation among co-workers of being excellent at human relations, it is okay for you to circle an 8, 9, or in a rare case, the 10. If you are frequently negative and it hurts your personal as well as group productivity, give yourself a 5 or under.

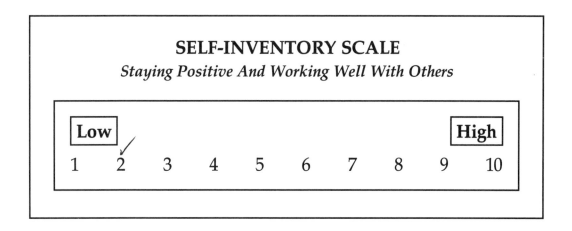

SELF-INVENTORY SCALE

Staying Positive And Working Well With Others

Low									High
1	2	3	4	5	6	7	8	9	10

Category 5

Are You Taking Yourself Too Seriously?

DEVELOPING A SENSE OF HUMOR

Some individuals have the capacity to take a serious situation and "flip it over" so they can find a humorous perspective that may lie underneath. When they find something that is laughable and then share it with others, everyone makes a better adjustment. In the world of work, such people are invaluable.

Humor, deep down inside, is an expression of joy that comes from being free. It is a form of communication. It is fun to laugh. According to many medical experts laughter is a therapeutic experience. But humor does not come as easily to some as it does to others. Thus, to develop a sense of humor requires an awareness of its value to the person who makes the effort. Please ask yourself these questions.

- Do you view humor as a way to enhance your career?

- Do you view telling laughable stories or jokes as a way of building better relationships with others?

- Do you feel that many people take life too seriously? Including yourself?

- What is your humor quotient? That is, just how good are you at dispensing humor?

To find an answer to the last question, please turn the page and continue.

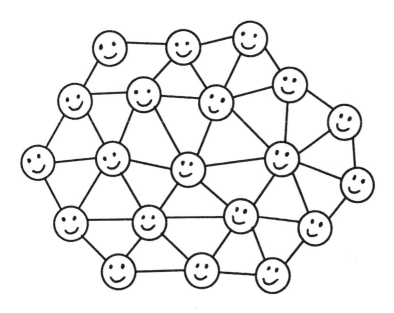

EXERCISE: HUMOR QUOTIENT*

Read the statements and circle the number where you feel you belong. If you circle a 7, you are saying the statement is ''very characteristic of you''; if you circle a 1, the statement is ''very uncharacteristic of you.'' Be honest—No one is watching!

1. My boss would describe me as a ''Humor Asset'' because my sense of humor benefits the company.   7 6 5 4 3 2 1

2. My co-workers and family would list my sense of humor as one of my best assets.   7 6 5 4 3 2 1

3. I avoid sarcasm, ethnic, or negative humor except in private conversations with close friends.   7 6 5 4 3 2 1

4. I can laugh at my own mistakes and enjoy occasionally being poked fun at.   7 6 5 4 3 2 1

5. I laugh alone when I feel something is funny.   7 6 5 4 3 2 1

6. As a humor consumer, I easily laugh and enjoy laughing at jokes and stories others share.   7 6 5 4 3 2 1

7. I seek out cartoons, comedy shows, comedians and other humor stimulants.   7 6 5 4 3 2 1

8. I write down humorous stories and keep cartoons and articles that promote humor.   7 6 5 4 3 2 1

9. When stressed on the job, my sense of humor helps me keep my perspective.   7 6 5 4 3 2 1

10. I spontaneously look for the funny side of life and share it with others.   7 6 5 4 3 2 1

11. I send humorous notes and cartoons to friends, co-workers, and customers.   7 6 5 4 3 2 1

12. My sense of humor makes it hard for people to stay mad at me.   7 6 5 4 3 2 1

13. I love to tell humorous stories to make my point in on-the-job communication.   7 6 5 4 3 2 1

14. I sometimes act silly at unexpected times.   7 6 5 4 3 2 1

15. I am not uncomfortable laughing out loud with co-workers.   7 6 5 4 3 2 1

16. I use humor to help myself and others recall important things.   7 6 5 4 3 2 1

If you score 100–112, you are lying or can't add; a score between 90–99, indicates ''Humor Pro''; a score of 70-90 means minor adjustments may be in order; a score of 45-70 suggests a major adjustment is needed; a score below 45 may require a ''humor transplant.'' If you did not laugh or smile at this scoring, give yourself a zero!

*This exercise was taken from the excellent book *Making Humor Work* by Terry Paulson. See the back of this book for details on how you might obtain this publication.

FUN IN THE WORKPLACE

Holding down a job is serious business. Building a career within the structure of a corporation is a demanding adventure. Productivity levels are important. To stay hired they must be maintained, and to advance they should be increased. Skills must be honed. Quality must be achieved. Work is work!

But all work, now and then, needs an injection of lightness for the following reasons.

- Employees can get so serious and tense that appropriate humor can increase productivity, not diminish it.
- Laughter among a working ''team'' will increase the spirit and motivation of all members.
- The right amount of humor can help create and maintain positive working relationships that benefit everyone.

A sense of humor is also necessary in building a successful career. That is why the editors of this book decided to include it as one of the twelve most important work qualities in the inventory (profile) on page 92.

You have probably known someone who is highly capable mentally, well-educated, and seems to have *everything*—but never reaches her or his potential. The reason? Often it is because of the missing ingredient—a sense of humor.

Whatever your career goal may be, you are encouraged to be a professional. But a professional without a sense of humor may not reach his or her goal—and will not have nearly as much fun getting there!

> *''There are three rules for creating humor, but unfortunately no one knows what they are.''*
> **Laurence Peter**

CASE STUDY

CASE NUMBER 8

Yesterday was a big event for Trisha because she was invited to be the manager of her department. The invitation took place when she and her manager were asked to meet with the Vice President of her division and the Director of Human Resources. The V.P. announced that she was the company choice for the promotion. Then the Director of Human Resources talked about her new salary and when she would attend her first management training seminar. Trisha was excited, it was a big day!

When the meeting ended, Trish thanked everyone and asked if a question would be in order. The group agreed, so she asked: "I'm curious as to why I was selected over others with more training and experience." Everyone looked to her supervisor for a answer. He replied: "It was your positive sense of humor."

Do you agree or disagree that a sense of humor is important enough to make the difference in selecting one candidate over another?

Turn to page 104 and compare your answer.

RATING YOURSELF ON HUMOR

Your Humor Quotient (page 36) indicates your ability to use humor. It does not necessarily measure how often you use humor, how successful you are at it, or what impact humor has on your attitude and job productivity. In completing the scale below, please analyze how you use humor in your workplace.

- Do you use as *much* humor as you should?

- Does your use of humor keep you from taking your job too seriously?

- Do you weave some form of humor into most of your conversations?

- Do you constantly *look* for humor in problem or negative situations?

- *Do you contribute significantly to team spirit through your sense of humor?*

If you rate yourself 8 or above, you are saying you make better use of humor than others in your work environment. If you rate yourself from 4 to 7, you are saying that you contribute your share. A rating of 3 or less is a signal that your humor quotient needs work.

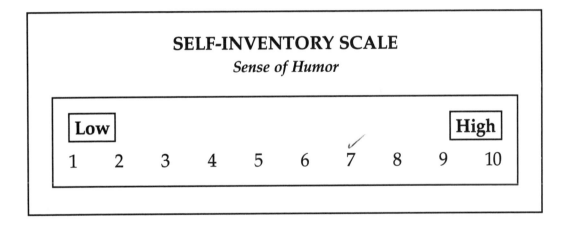

SELF-INVENTORY SCALE
Sense of Humor

Low									High
1	2	3	4	5	6	7	8	9	10

Category 6

Does Your Attitude Need A Positive Boost?

THE NEED FOR FREQUENT ATTITUDE RENEWAL

Everyone—employees, students, homemakers, retirees—must occasionally engage in some form of attitude renewal or adjustment. There is no escape.

Renewal means to restore or refresh your view; rejuvenate your approach; reestablish your positive focus; and/or repair the damage of wear and tear to your attitude.

Weekends, holidays, and vacation periods are frequently used as ''pit stops'' for attitude adjustment purposes. They are necessary to combat the following:

1. *External shock waves.* As a seismograph records the intensity and duration of an earthquake, your attitude reflects tremors caused by financial reversals, personal disappointments, family problems, health concerns, and so on. There is no way to fully insulate yourself from these shock waves.

2. *Self-image problems.* We frequently become critical of the way we appear to ourselves. Maybe we have put on a few pounds—or are not as well-groomed as in the past. This creates a negative self-image—a kind of dirty lens that keeps us from thinking of ourselves in a positive way. When this happens, working on a better image is mandatory. Health clubs, clothing stores, fashion boutiques, barber and beauty shops are, in effect, attitude adjustment stations.

3. *Negative drift.* Nobody can explain why it happens, but sometimes, even when the environment is calm and you have a good self-image, there can be a movement toward a negative attitude. Some blame this drift on the negative aspects in today's society. The feeling is that because you are bombarded with so many negative stimuli through news stories, you tend to become more negative by osmosis.

Regardless of the reason—environmental shock waves, self-image problems or negative drift—everyone needs to adjust his or her attitude on occasion.

Attitude renewal at the first level is a daily process. For some, a few moments of meditation may be the answer. Others, who seem to get off to a bad start, have learned to call a friend mid-morning for a ''boost.'' Still others use music or comedy as part of their daily routine.

WHAT IS A POSITIVE ATTITUDE?*

On the surface, attitude is the way you communicate your mood to others. When you are optimistic and anticipate successful encounters, you transmit a positive attitude and people usually respond favorably. When you are pessimistic and expect the worst, your attitude often is negative; and people tend to avoid you. Inside your head, where it all starts, attitude is a mind set. *It is the way you look at things mentally.*

Think of attitude as your mental focus on the outside world. Like using a camera, you can focus or set your mind on what appeals to you.* You can see situations as either opportunities or failures: a cold winter day as either beautiful or ugly, a departmental meeting as interesting or boring. Perception—the complicated process of viewing and interpreting your environment—is a mental phenomenon. It is within your power to concentrate on selected aspects of your environment and ignore others. Quite simply, you take the picture of life you want to take.

Emphasizing the positive and diffusing the negative is like using a magnifying glass. You can place the glass over good news and feel better, or you can magnify bad news and make yourself miserable. Magnifying situations can become a habit. If you continually focus on difficult situations, the result will be exaggerated distortions of problems. A better approach might be to imagine you have binoculars. Use the magnifying end to view positive things, and reverse them (using the other end) whenever you encounter negative elements—to make them appear smaller. Once you are able to alter your imagery to highlight the positive, you are on the right road.

THE CHALLENGE OF STAYING POSITIVE

Attitude is never static. It is an on-going dynamic, sensitive, perceptual process. Unless you are on constant guard, negative factors can slip into your perspective. This will cause you to spend ''mind time'' on difficulties rather than opportunities.

If negative factors stay around long enough, they will be reflected in your disposition. The positive is still there, but it has been overshadowed by the negative.

It is a challenge to push the negative factors to the outer perimeter of your thinking. Those who learn this ''trick,'' will reflect it, and others will notice.

Of course, no one can be positive all of the time. Excessive optimism—like Pollyanna in the novels by Eleanor Porter—is not realistic. Friends and business associates will probably feel it is plastic. After all, a positive attitude is not an act; it must be genuine. Sometimes, when things get really tough, a positive attitude may be impossible, or even inappropriate. The ''we shall overcome'' perspective is more determination based upon rightful indignation than that of a positive attitude.

When things are going well, a positive attitude becomes self-reinforcing and easy to maintain. Being human, however, insures that something will always happen to test your positive mind set. Some person or situation is always on the horizon to step on your attitude and challenge your ability to bounce back.

YOU KEEP YOUR POSITIVE ATTITUDE WHEN YOU GIVE IT AWAY

When you are frustrated by the behavior of others, you may be tempted to give them "a piece of your mind." This is understandable. It is a better policy, however, to give them "a piece of your positive attitude." When you do this, it allows others to adjust your attitude for you.

> Sharon asked Casey to meet her for lunch because she needed a psychological lift. Casey didn't feel like it, but she accepted and made a special effort to be upbeat. When the luncheon was over, Casey had not only given Sharon a boost, she felt better herself. Both parties came out ahead.

When you give a part of your positive attitude to others, you create a symbiotic relationship. The recipient feels better, but so do you. It is interesting but true that *you keep your positive attitude by giving it away*.

When it comes to giving your positive attitude to others, you can be generous and selfish at the same time.

> Mrs. Lindsey is considered a master teacher. The primary reason is because she freely shares her positive attitude with students and colleagues. In return, students and fellow teachers are constantly reinforcing Mrs. Lindsey's attitude with compliments and attention.
>
> Mr. Trent is an outstanding office manager. He is also a tease. Every day he creates a little levity to balance the pressure of work. In sharing his good humor he is rewarded by a dedicated staff that works hard to deliver higher productivity because they appreciate the pleasant work environment.

CASE STUDIES

CASE NUMBER 9

At Shannon's last performance review her supervisor gave her a ''fair'' rating on attitude instead of good or excellent. Shannon thought she deserved better and challenged the rating. During the discussion that followed, her supervisor said she felt Shannon could be more friendly with clients, patient with co-workers, upbeat on the telephone, and also be more communicative.

The rating was not changed and, as a result, Shannon almost resigned. But, after talking it over with her husband, she decided maybe her supervisor was sending her a message, so she decided to change her focus and concentrate on being more positive. Three months later her husband said: ''Shannon, I have noticed a major improvement in our relationship. You are more fun than in the past and all of our friends are talking about it.''

Is it possible for an attitude change in one environment (work) to improve one's focus in another environment (social)?

Compare your views with that of the author on page 104.

ASSESSING YOUR ATTITUDE

Assessing someone else's attitude is a sensitive and dangerous undertaking as Shannon's supervisor discovered. It is also difficult to assess your own attitude. We all have a tendency to feel we are more positive than other people may interpret us to be.

Before completing the 1 to 10 scale below, please ask yourself:

- Do you see yourself as a highly positive person with only occasional down periods?

- Over the long haul, are you measurably more positive than other co-workers?

- Do you consider your positive attitude to be your most priceless possession?

- Do co-workers sometimes ask you: "How do you manage to stay so positive?"

If you gave yourself "yes" answers to the above questions, do not hesitate to circle the 8, 9, or possibly, the 10. If you sense you can be measurably more positive in the future, circle a lower number.

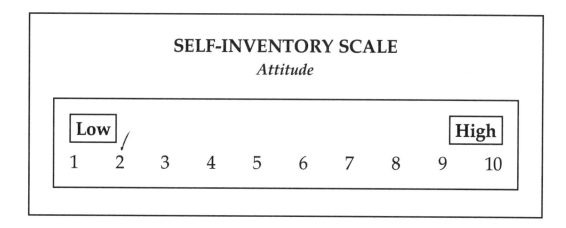

SELF-INVENTORY SCALE
Attitude

Low									High
1	2	3	4	5	6	7	8	9	10

Category 7

Are You Sufficiently Assertive?

NONASSERTIVE

ASSERTIVE

AGGRESSIVE

HOW TO DEVELOP POSITIVE ASSERTIVENESS

It would be nice if you could simply decide to go down the road marked ''Assertive'' and live your life without straying from the path.

Real life is full of twists and turns and *no one is consistently assertive*. All of us use the three basic behavior styles described below depending on the situation and personal factors. The good news is that *we can learn to become more assertive more of the time*.

1. NONASSERTIVE behavior is passive and indirect. It communicates a message of inferiority. By being nonassertive we allow the wants, needs, and rights of others to be more important than our own. Nonassertive behavior helps create ''win-lose'' situations. A person behaving nonassertively will lose while allowing others to win (or at best be disregarded). Following this road leads to being a victim, not a winner.

2. AGGRESSIVE behavior is more complex. It can be either active or passive. Aggression can be direct or indirect, honest or dishonest—but it always communicates an impression of superiority and disrespect. By being aggressive we put our wants, needs, and rights above those of others. We attempt to get our way by not allowing others a choice. Aggressive behavior is usually inappropriate because it violates the rights of others. People behaving aggressively may ''win'' by making sure others ''lose''—but in doing so set themselves up for retaliation. No one likes a bully.

3. ASSERTIVE behavior is active, direct, and honest. It communicates an impression of self-respect and respect for others. By being assertive we view our wants, needs, and rights as equal with those of others. We work toward ''win-win'' outcomes. An assertive person wins by influencing, listening, and negotiating so that others choose to cooperate willingly. This behavior leads to success without retaliation and encourages honest, open relationships!

EXERCISE: AN ASSERTIVENESS QUIZ

Before learning how to develop your assertiveness, it is important to take a few moments to get some idea of where you are right now. Answer the questions below honestly. They will help you gain some insights about your current level of assertiveness.

Assign a number to each item using this scale:

ALWAYS				NEVER
5	4	3	2	1

_____ 1. I ask others to do things without feeling guilty or anxious.

_____ 2. When someone asks me to do something I don't want to do, I say "no" without feeling guilty or anxious.

_____ 3. I am comfortable when speaking to a large group of people.

_____ 4. I confidently express my honest opinions to authority figures (such as my boss).

_____ 5. When I experience powerful feelings (anger, frustration, disappointment, etc.), I verbalize them easily.

_____ 6. When I express anger, I do so without blaming others for "making me mad."

_____ 7. I am comfortable speaking up in a group situation.

_____ 8. If I disagree with the majority opinion in a meeting, I can "stick to my guns" without feeling uncomfortable or being abrasive.

_____ 9. When I make a mistake, I will acknowledge it.

_____ 10. I tell others when their behavior creates a problem for me.

_____ 11. Meeting new people in social situations is something I do with ease and comfort.

_____ 12. When discussing my beliefs, I do so without labeling the opinions of others as "crazy," "stupid," "ridiculous," "irrational."

_____ 13. I assume that most people are competent and trustworthy and do not have difficulty delegating tasks to others.

_____ 14. When considering doing something I have never done, I feel confident I can learn to do it.

_____ 15. I believe my needs are as important as those of others and I am entitled to have my needs satisfied.

TOTAL SCORE (Sum of the 15 numbers)

If your total is 60 or higher, you have a consistently assertive philosophy and probably handle most situations well. If your total is 45–60 you have a fairly assertive outlook. If your total is 30–45, your natural response is often nonassertive or aggressive. If your total is 15–30 you have considerable difficulty being assertive.

CASE STUDIES

CASE NUMBER 10

Assume your name is Alice, and Kim Aoki, who was raised and educated in Japan, has become one of your best friends. You work closely together in corporate headquarters. Kim is excellent in computer programming, dealing with accounting systems, and her English is impeccable. But she is having trouble adjusting to the United States culture.

Kim is quiet, unassuming, and quickly moves to the background when her position is challenged by others. Last night the two of you were discussing the problem in an open but probing way. When you ask Kim why she finds it so difficult to stand up for herself, she replies: "It is the way I was raised. I feel uncomfortable when there are confrontations of any kind." You reply: "How might I help you?" Kim says: "I just want to be more assertive, more like you."

How would you go about helping Kim?

CASE NUMBER 11

Joanne is outstanding when it comes to setting up office procedures that take advantage of available computer technology. As a result, she is successful despite her abrasive way in working with people. Management puts up with Joanne because she gets the job done, but closer observation would signal that she leaves a wake of unhappy and less productive employees behind. As one co-worker put it: "Joanne took an assertiveness seminar and she turned out to be aggressive. She has great potential but few people want to be around her."

If you were Joanne's supervisor, how would you go about reversing the process so that she would turn her overbearing manner into a natural and pleasant assertiveness?

Turn to page 104 for author's comments on both cases.

ASSERTIVENESS SELF-IMPROVEMENT SCALE

It may be more difficult to rate yourself on assertiveness than any of the other eleven factors involved in the profile. Why? Because you circle the highest number only if you feel you have the exact balance between aggressiveness and nonassertiveness. For example, if you frequently demonstrate aggressive behavior (such as getting emotionally involved to the point you over-talk, push people around, or generally disregard the needs of others), you should not circle any number higher than a 5. On the other hand, if you are nonassertive so that you are often ignored while others are consulted, here, again you should not circle any number higher than a 5.

However, if you sincerely believe you are not nonassertive and not aggressive, you can rate yourself somewhere above 5.

- If you feel you have just the right degree of assertiveness, give yourself a 9 or 10.

- If you are pleased with your assertiveness but know there is some room for improvement, circle the number 7 or 8.

- If you are not pleased with your progress toward the degree of assertiveness you believe to be right for you, circle the 6 or lower.

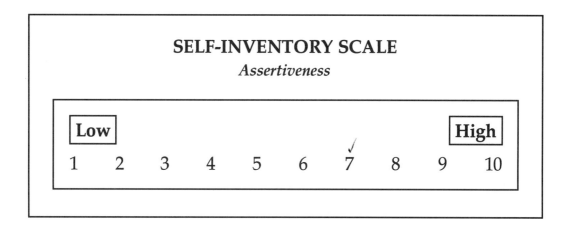

Category 8

Do Your Job Skills Need To Be Upgraded?

THE WINDS OF CHANGE

Not only do organizations change (restructuring) but the jobs within them also have new dimensions. This is especially true when the positions are technical by nature and must, therefore, improve when new technology arrives. Job descriptions these days seldom remain static for more than a few months.

What does this mean to the individual who occupies the position? It means those who wish to be successful must stay flexible and open to new experiences.

- It may mean additional training, either on the job or in a special class.

- It may mean attending a company-sponsored seminar.

- It may mean engaging in a self-help program with the assistance of a manual or new machine.

All jobs have certain skills that need to be upgraded frequently. New equipment, supplies, procedures, or techniques all need to be mastered as soon as possible. It is difficult to find a job where additional training is not required or desirable.

What does it all mean? It means that skill or competency upgrading is a constant responsibility of the worker. Those who accept the challenge prepare themselves for advancement; those who reject the challenge find themselves shuffled into less demanding jobs. As long as the winds of change are blowing, re-training, skill upgrading, and new approaches to excellence will be in vogue.

It is necessary for organizational survival!

EXERCISE: MEASURING THE DEGREE OF CHANGE IN YOUR JOB

Some jobs change faster than others do. For example, those connected with the computer or communication industries must change quickly to keep up with the new technology; those employed in some service occupations (selling, food preparation, delivery) usually change at a slower pace, but change nonetheless.

What about the job you currently occupy? To discover the speed at which it is changing please answer the following questions.

	Yes	No
1. Are you operating any new equipment from one year ago?	____	____
2. Have some co-workers passed you as far as selected skills are concerned?	____	____
3. Do you find yourself asking others to bring you up-to-date on new procedures or techniques?	____	____
4. Has your attitude toward change become more negative in recent months?	____	____
5. Are you avoiding methods to upgrade your skills even when you know it would be smart for you to do so?	____	____
6. Are you uncomfortable with the number of mistakes you are making?	____	____
7. Have you given up on getting a promotion because you recognize your skills are no longer up to par?	____	____
8. Has there been a decrease in your producitivity because of changes in your job specifications?	____	____
9. Do you sense you are falling behind others in the skill-competency race?	____	____
10. Has your superior suggested that you sign up for either a company-sponsored seminar or return to school for upgrading purposes?	____	____

If you gave seven or more YES answers, it would appear that you should make immediate arrangements to profit from some additional training. If you gave five, six, or seven YES answers, the need is less urgent. If you gave four or fewer YES answers, you appear to be keeping up with the competency requirements of your profession.

CASE STUDY

CASE NUMBER 12

Felicia is sick and tired of having to improve her computer skills all of the time. She no sooner becomes comfortable with one machine or piece of software when here comes something new. All she wants, really, is a job that is not over-demanding so she can save her mental and physical energy for her family and personal life.

Yesterday, to her surprise, Felicia was offered an opportunity to become a supervisor in her department. Ah, she thought, this is for me. I can keep good relationships with everyone but I can delegate all the skill stuff to others who like it more than I do. I will also have more freedom.

Is Felicia making a logical decision?

To match your thoughts with that of the author turn to page 104.

SKILL LEVEL SCALE

You are now invited to rate yourself on how well you have mastered the skills that are required in your present job. Such skills or competencies might include the quality of your written communications, skills connected with a computer, mechanical skills, financial or accounting skills, etc. A job description usually includes these or other specific skills required for top performance in a job.

In rating yourself, keep in mind that you are comparing your skill level (speed, accuracy, depth, etc.) with others in similar jobs *only*. Also include the skill in which you deal with customers, either in person or on the telephone. Few people reach a 10 level, but a score of 1, 2, or 3 may mean you are on probation until your skill level is increased.

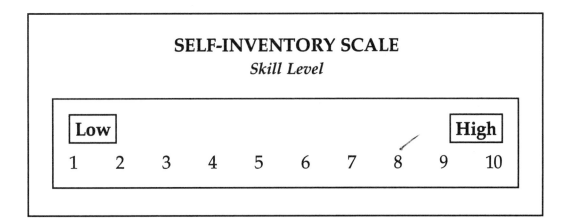

Category 9

Are You Satisfied With The Quality Of Your Work?

THE SWITCH TO EXCELLENCE

There has been a noticeable movement in the direction of higher quality products and improved service in the past few years. The pursuit of excellence is a reality. There are four major reasons for this trend.

- Product safety has been highlighted by consumer advocate groups and legal implications have followed.

- Organizations have become more aware of their environmental and social responsibilities.

- Repeat sales depend more upon customer satisfaction (quality) than in the past.

- International competition has set higher quality standards with some products.

All of this has caused higher management to place a greater emphasis on quality. Law enforcement personnel are expected to be more aware of the rights and privileges of others, registered nurses are expected to make fewer mistakes in dispensing drugs; restaurant servers are expected to explain the menu better; computer and correspondence mistakes are not accepted with the easy tolerance of the past. As a popular television commercial communicates: Quality Is Job One!

Sacrificing quality for speed or total output has always been a questionable policy. Now almost everyone accepts the belief that it is better to stay as close as possible to zero defect quality standards before concentrating on speed or output. This quality first, speed second philosophy has been shown to improve the profit picture of the organization. Especially in the long run.

EXERCISE: QUALITY QUESTIONNAIRE

This exercise is designed to measure your attitude toward quality work as opposed to average standards. *Quality is a frame of mind.* Some organizations are more successful in getting high quality work from their employees than others.

Please place a check (✔) under YES or NO for each statement.

	Yes	No

1. I would take personal pride in working for a firm that demands quality standards. ____ ____

2. I feel good about doing something right even if it is routine work, and I must perform the same function over and over again. ____ ____

3. I like being orderly, organized, and efficient. It bothers me to make a mistake. ____ ____

4. I would rather be reprimanded for being slow than sloppy. ____ ____

5. I have little patience with anyone who has a ''get by'' attitude. ____ ____

6. Speed is to be admired in any job as long as quality is not sacrificed. ____ ____

7. I would rather re-do a lengthy report on my own time than submit it with a single error. ____ ____

8. You can't call yourself a professional in any job unless you put quality first. ____ ____

9. I believe in the two phrases ''haste makes waste'' and ''safety first.'' ____ ____

10. I enjoy doing things right even if no one will know about it but me. ____ ____

The more YES answers you gave yourself the more positive your attitude is toward quality work. Five NO answers may be a signal that the quality of your efforts could show improvement.

CASE STUDY

CASE NUMBER 13

Victor has the mental capacity to move in many directions at the same time and still do a better than average job on most projects. But he occasionally moves so fast that, along the way, quality suffers. You are Victor's superior and you would like to prepare him as your replacement. He has outstanding leadership ability. The only major characteristic that bothers you is his willingness to sacrifice a small degree of excellence.

You devise three separate strategies which you feel might convince Victor that quality will make him more valuable to the company—and also more promotable. Your strategies are:

Strategy 1: Construct an imaginary case that demonstrates how quality took a person into a top management circle ahead of others. Discuss it with Victor.

Strategy 2: Explain why your CEO is such an advocate of excellence through a discussion of the firm's expressed mission—EXCELLENCE ABOVE ALL.

Strategy 3: Tell a story on yourself where you made a serious mistake by not putting quality ahead of everything else.

Which strategy would you employ to convince Victor? Why?

Compare with author's response on page 105.

QUALITY WORK PERFORMANCE SCALE

Now that you have expressed yourself regarding quality work standards, please rate yourself on the quality aspects of your current performance in the job *you hold now*. As you do this on the scale below, please keep the following in mind:

- A 10 rating means quality perfection which may be impossible to achieve in most jobs.

- A 1 rating means you have no concern for quality. "Getting by" without getting caught is your goal.

- A 5 rating means you are average in quality work performance for YOUR KIND OF JOB IN YOUR FIRM.

Be as honest and objective as possible. Circle the number that reflects your actual performance, not what you hope it will be in the future.

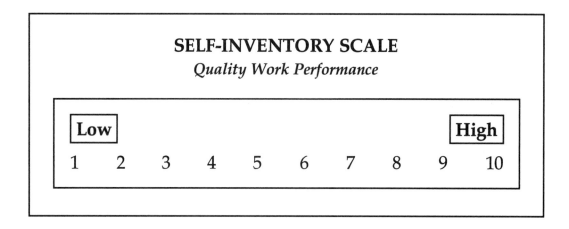

Category 10

Do You Have Your Career And Lifestyle Organized?

SELF-MANAGEMENT IS THE KEY

According to Dr. Paul M. Timm, author of *Successful Self-Management,* an acceptable definition of self-management would be:

> The *process* of maximizing our *time and talents* to achieve *worthwhile goals* while achieving a *balanced life*.

Note the key words:

Process: Self-management is ongoing. It is not something we do only once or occasionally. We make it a process by adopting some simple ''rituals'' or ''routines'' into our daily lives.

Time and Talents: These are unique personal resources that we alone can manage. In essence, it is *through* our time and talent that we manage people, finances, etc.

Worthwhile Goals: These are the outcomes of our efforts—our planned-for achievements. Our rewards! To be truly worthwhile, such goals must be rooted in a sound value system.

Balanced Life: A primary challenge is managing our careers in such a way that we have time to manage our personal lifestyles and leisure time. In other words, organized people find greater fulfillment in their personal lives.

In summary, self-management is more than *just* making the best use of our time. It is making maximum use of our talents by setting daily, weekly, monthly, and longer-term goals and proceeding to reach them through various self-management techniques.

THE NUTS AND BOLTS OF TIME AND TASK MANAGEMENT

Most time management experts agree that rule number one in a thoughtful planning process is some form of notebook calendar, or planner where you can write things down.

How much time should you devote to daily planning? It will vary with each individual, but a minimum of 10 or 15 minutes a day solely devoted to planning is recommended. Use the steps described below and you should see a significant increase in your personal effectiveness.*

How to Do Effective Daily Task Planning

1. *Develop a priority task list for each day.* Prioritizing tasks helps us sort them out, determine which need to be attacked first, and which can be saved for later.

2. *Assign a letter priority to each item on your list.* Use **A**, **B**, **C**, or ★ (star) and put the letter **A** next to items that *MUST* be done. These are critical to you. You alone determine whether they are critical or not. This decision is based on your values and goals. Tasks required either by outside forces (like your boss) or internal ones (such as a personal commitment) will normally receive an **A** priority.

   Use the letter **B** to indicate *SHOULD DO* items. These are things that should be done, items that are really worth spending time on. They aren't quite as critical as the **A**'s, but they're nevertheless important.

   The letter **C** is for *COULD DO* items. These are things worth listing, and worth thinking about. And if you get the **A**'s and **B**'s completed, worth doing.

   A **star** ★ indicates an item that is *URGENT*—something that *must* be done *now!* It is both important and vital. You've got to get on it right away. These items occasionally come up during a work day. When you add them to your list, put a star by them, and drop whatever else you're doing, even if it's an **A** item— and complete that task.

3. *Assign a number to your tasks.* You can further sharpen your plan of attack by assigning a number to each task.

   Use the numbering system as a chronological indicator. That is, ask which task should I realistically do first? If I have a meeting at two in the afternoon and it's an **A** item, it may not be **A-1**, simply because there are other things to do earlier in the day. As with other priorities, you decide how to best use it, but a number system will provide your marching orders.

CASE STUDY

CASE NUMBER 14   *RICA AND ROLPH*

Rica leaves her job each afternoon without a plan for the following day. Her strategy is to free herself from work responsibilities quickly so that she can pursue her personal lifestyle. In defense of her pattern, Rica claims she is so wiped out by the end of the day that planning ahead would be ineffective. However, as soon as she is in the middle of her 40 minute commute the next morning, she thinks about her plans for the day. She often uses a notebook to organize her thoughts.

Rolph is always the last to leave work, usually thirty minutes after his last employee has left. A highly organized person, he finishes up on many details and then quietly sets down his priorities for the following day on his desk calendar. Rolph claims this helps him to leave all work problems behind so he can enjoy his lifestyle to the fullest. He doesn't think about business until he shows up at his desk the following morning.

Which plan would work best for you? Is your present plan superior?

_____

_____

_____

See author's preference on page 105.

CASE STUDY

CASE NUMBER 15 *DARLENE*

Darlene, a single parent, is most efficient and is respected as an office manager. Over the years, she has learned and applied the techniques of self-management to her career with outstanding results. With her Time-Planning Notebook at hand, she makes maximum use of her time and achieves high standards of quality from her employees.

Things are very different in her personal life. For some reason, she refuses to apply her self-management techniques at home. Results? Her home is such a mess she refuses to invite friends to drop by. She is always having breakdowns with her car due to lack of maintenance. And without an organized wardrobe her appearance often leaves much to be desired. Worst of all, she does not follow a diet and is seriously overweight.

When a close friend, Shelly, recently suggested to Darlene that she was making a mistake by not applying her self-management techniques to her lifestyle, she replied: ''Shell, down deep inside I hate being an organized person. Somehow, it causes me to tighten up and lose my sense of joy and creativity. I force myself to be organized in my career because I couldn't hold a management job without it, but when the work-day is over I need the relaxation that comes from being disorganized. I guess, for me, it is a kind of balance to keep my sanity.''

Do you agree with Darlene? If you were Shelly, what argument would you advance to convince her she should apply her self-management techniques at home?

_____

_____

_____

Turn to page 105 to compare your thoughts with those of the author.

SELF-MANAGEMENT EVALUATION

Some people manage themselves in a quiet, efficient, systematic, and consistent manner. In so doing, they accomplish their professional and personal goals. These individuals take great pride in being organized and they enjoy the process. They should rate themselves an 8 or higher.

Other people seem to manage themselves rather well but do it reluctantly and inconsistently. They force the process and do not enjoy it. They should rate themselves somewhere between 4 and 7.

Still others let other people and their environment manage *them*. Circumstances dictate their behavior. Their job activities and personal lives are helter-skelter. The results usually spell career stagnation or worse. These individuals should rate themselves 4 or under.

SELF-INVENTORY SCALE
Self-Management

Low									High
1	2	3	4	5	6	7	8	9	10

Category 11

Are You Reaching Your Creativity Potential?

EVERYONE HAS A CREATIVITY POTENTIAL

It may come as a surprise to you that creativity is included as one of the twelve self-improvement categories. Many people, unfortunately, feel that creativity is confined to those with artistic talent or the ability to think on a conceptual level beyond the average individual. Not so. Everyone has the potential to be creative in their own way.

Creativity in the work environment is any thought that manifests itself into a suggestion that will increase productivity. Often simple ideas are the best. Doing something only slightly differently can produce a saving in the use of paper, or improve employee morale, or increase efficiency through the rearranging of office furniture. Of course, creativity can also include more complex ideas that improve the quality of products, and service to customers, and at the same time solve major problems. The point is that creativity is not limited to selected individuals or blockbuster ideas.

It is easy to recognize the desirability for creativity in an advertising agency. Yet, creativity can be equally important in a shipping department or office job.

You might conclude that your job is non-creative because it involves mostly routine tasks. If so, take a second look. You may be passing up some excellent opportunities to contribute some imaginative ideas and along the way improve your career advancement possibilities.

In the past, some organizations have encouraged suggestions from employees by offering prizes or placing suggestion boxes around the facility. A better approach might be to distribute "creativity envelopes" along with paychecks so ideas could be submitted to obtain special rewards and recognition. All suggestions spring from creative roots!

MORE GREEN, PABLO

CASE STUDY

CASE NUMBER 16   *JERRY*

When in college Jerry was always referred to as the ''idea guy'' by his friends. Some of Jerry's ideas were really off the wall. Others were down to earth and practical. Everyone figured he would wind up doing movies or some kind of highly creative work.

In Jerry's first job with a large marketing firm, he took three months getting the lay of the land. Then, almost every week, he would submit a marketing idea—one connected with packaging, buying incentives, or how to improve sales via the various media. All of his ideas were submitted verbally to his supervisor, Sally North. After more than two months and not having heard anything about his ideas, he confronted Ms. North. Her reply was: ''The first time I get an idea from you that shows maturity, you will have my support.''

Two months and about six good ideas without a response later, Jerry decided on a new strategy. Instead of submitting his ideas verbally, he would present them in a creative manner (special art, etc.) to both Ms. North and her superior. In Jerry's mind, this in itself would show creativity as well as bring attention to his ideas.

What is your opinion of Jerry's strategy?

_____

_____

_____

_____

See page 105 for comments from the author.

CREATIVITY ASSESSMENT

Your challenge on this page is to do your best in evaluating your creative contributions during the past year. To assist you in doing this, please ask yourself these questions.

- Have you been underestimating your creative nature and, as a result, making fewer creative contributions that otherwise would be the case?

- Is your failure to make more creative suggestions slowing your career progress?

- Have you had ideas at work that you feel would improve productivity but failed to submit them?

- Has your mind produced some creative ideas that you kept to yourself?

- Would a "second look" at your present job show more creative opportunities than you have seen in the past?

If you have been going along without using your creative powers, rate yourself a 5 or under. If, however, you have been using your creativity to improve your job or the productivity of your department, rate yourself higher. If you have been improving your present job, helping to develop a better department, and on top of that submitting creative ideas to improve your company as a whole, give yourself a 9 or a 10.

SELF-INVENTORY SCALE
Creativity

Low								High	
1	2	3	4	5	6	7	8	9	10

Category 12

Can You Stop Procrastinating?

ARE YOU A PROCRASTINATOR?*

Millions of people, with otherwise good intentions, postpone important things they know they should be doing. You're one of them if you respond positively to each of the following statements: (Be truthful.)

1. I know who and what I am...but I want something better!

2. I'm frustrated because I can't do everything I want to do.

3. I'm delaying an important task I know I should be working on and that bothers me. (Your task could be: asking for a raise, finishing a report, calling on a prospect, starting a new career, studying for an examination, etc.). Add your own:

   My Task: _____

4. My task is important because this is what will happen if I don't do it:

   The Consequence: _____

   _____

5. My task has a beginning, an ending, and a definite outcome (e.g., making a sale, getting a raise, producing a document).

   The Beginning: _____

   The Ending: _____

   The Specific Outcome: _____

6. There is a specific day, month, hour, or year on which I hope to have my task completed and I know what's early and what's late.

   The Completion Date: _____

7. I am deliberately doing something else to avoid my task (e.g., eating, drinking, sleeping, playing dead, playing tennis, doing busywork). Add your own:

   My Delaying Tactics: _____

8. I know in my heart that I really should be doing this task and I feel guilty about not doing it.

   Yes _____   No _____

---

*The material presented in this section is from the book *Stop Procrastinating* by James R. Sherman, Ph.D. It is highly recommended for anyone, but for those who habitually procrastinate, it is a must.

EXERCISE: MAJOR CAUSES OF PROCRASTINATION

The causes that follow aren't listed in any particular order of magnitude or importance. Check those that cause you to procrastinate.

☐ Confusion

☐ Lack of Priorities

☐ Lack of Responsibility

☐ Fear of Risk-Taking

☐ Escape from Unpleasant Tasks

☐ Anxiety or Depression

☐ Obsessive/Compulsive Behavior

☐ Monotony or Boredom

☐ Fatigue

☐ Outside Distractions

☐ Lack of Analytical Ability

☐ Forgetfulness

☐ Dependence on Others

☐ Manipulation of Others

☐ Physical Disabilities

ADD YOUR OWN:

☐ _____

☐ _____

HOW TO STOP PROCRASTINATING FOR GOOD

Are you angry and frustrated? Do you routinely have delays and postponements that keep you from reaching your goals and objectives? If so, then here's a simple, straightforward procedure that will help you break the procrastination habit and get you moving on the road to success.

Take these four steps and put an end to procrastination once and for all:

1. Acknowledge the simple fact that you procrastinate. Then make up your mind to stop doing it.

   I have procrastinated in the past, but I'm not going to do it anymore.

   Signed: _____

   Date: _____

2. Learn as much as you can about procrastination.

   • Recognize what it is.

   • Figure out why you do it.

   • Find out what you can do to stop.

3. Make a list of specific things you're going to start doing right away to break this lousy habit.

   First, I'm going to: _____

   Then, I'll: _____

   Finally, I'll: _____

4. Carry out your plan of action.

> "Try not," said Yoda, the Jedi Master. "Do. Or do not. There is no try."
> *"The Empire Strikes Back"*
> George Lucas

Commit yourself to getting rid of procrastination and do it now!

CASE STUDY

Jess is forever taking seminars and reading self-help books in an effort to improve himself. Once finished, he vows he will improve in that area. The only problem is that within a few days, he is back into his old pattern and no permanent behavioral changes have been accomplished.

As his supervisor, you decide to give Jess a system that will help Jess to change his behavior so he can take advantage of what he learns. The system is a simple one. It recommends that having completed a seminar or self-help book, Jess write down from five to seven changes he would like to make. Never less than five or more than seven. Then, after three days, you go over Jess's list with him, asking which changes are most important? After selecting the one that Jess is convinced will do the most for him, have him write a big red checkmark next to it.

You instruct Jess to make the change checked an all-consuming objective for an entire week. Concentrate on it. Talk about it. Change habits to accommodate it.

Then, once Jess feels he has made the change permanent, he can go back to his original list and select another change or wait until another idea comes from a different source. Your motto is: ONE IMPORTANT CHANGE AT A TIME!

Will the change system work for Jess?

See page 105 for author's comments.

DON'T POSTPONE THIS RATING

You have now appraised your personal and career status in eleven significant areas. It is time for you to rate yourself on *how much initiative you normally demonstrate*. Obviously, if you are known as a procrastinator you deserve a low rating (5 or under) on this scale. But if you are not a procrastinator, how should you rate yourself?

- If you feel you could *modestly improve* your present level of initiative, circle the 5 or 6.

- If you are a real "self-starter" but could still demonstrate *more* initiative, circle the 7 or 8.

- If you rarely procrastinate and have the reputation as a "doer" with great follow-through, circle the 9 or 10.

As you rate yourself, keep in mind that you will have a few weak areas in your profile that will demand action on your part. If you circle a 7 or higher on this scale, you are committing yourself to do something about discovered weaknesses. Are you willing to do this?

SELF-INVENTORY SCALE
Initiative

Low									High
1	2	3	4	5	6	7	8	9	10

II

Constructing Your Profile

STEPS TO TAKE: VISUALIZING YOUR STRENGTHS AND WEAKNESSES

Now that you have rated yourself in the twelve critical self-improvement areas, you can begin building your personal profile so you can gain a better perspective regarding your strengths and weaknesses.

1. Study the profile sheet on the next two pages. Notice the twelve categories at the top, the scale from 1 to 10 on the left, and the squares at the bottom with page numbers assigned.

2. Return to the exercises you completed and record the numbers (from 1 to 10) that you recorded.

3. On the left part of the scale, locate the level on the column that equals the number at the bottom. Place a dot at this point.

4. Connect the dots or fill in the bar graph and you have completed your profile.

INVENTORY PROFILE SHEET

	SELF-ESTEEM	LEVEL OF WELLNESS	COMMUNICATIONS	QUALITY OF RELATIONSHIPS	SENSE OF HUMOR	ATTITUDE
HIGH 10						
9						
8						
7						
6						
5						
4						
3						
2						
LOW 1						
Rating						
Page Numbers	9	17	24	31	39	48

ASSERTIVENESS	LEVEL OF JOB SKILLS	QUALITY OF PERFORMANCE	SELF-MANAGEMENT	CREATIVITY	DEGREE OF INITIATIVE	
						10 HIGH
						9
						8
						7
						6
						5
						4
						3
						2
						1 LOW
						Rating
54	59	66	73	79	87	Page Numbers

SAMPLE
INVENTORY PROFILE SHEET
"DAN"

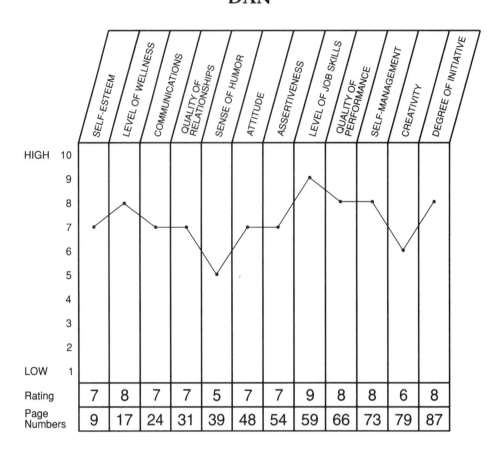

	SELF-ESTEEM	LEVEL OF WELLNESS	COMMUNICATIONS	QUALITY OF RELATIONSHIPS	SENSE OF HUMOR	ATTITUDE	ASSERTIVENESS	LEVEL OF JOB SKILLS	QUALITY OF PERFORMANCE	SELF-MANAGEMENT	CREATIVITY	DEGREE OF INITIATIVE
Rating	7	8	7	7	5	7	7	9	8	8	6	8
Page Numbers	9	17	24	31	39	48	54	59	66	73	79	87

INTERPRETATION:

- This profile suggests that Dan is highly conscientious, productive, and dependable but takes himself too seriously in the work environment. As a result, five categories—self-creativity, esteem, communications, relationships, attitude, and assertiveness suffer moderately.

- Humor is Dan's most critical weakness.

- Learning to laugh at the humorous side of work would have many benefits including: (1) better relationships with co-workers, (2) greater contribution to "team spirit," and (3) more recognition from management.

- It is unusual to find a profile with such a low rating in the humor category and a good rating in attitude. There is normally a symbiotic relationship between humor and attitude—one contributing to the improvement of the other. This may be an indication that Dan has a good sense of humor but does not express it openly.

SAMPLE
INVENTORY PROFILE SHEET
"BEVERLY"

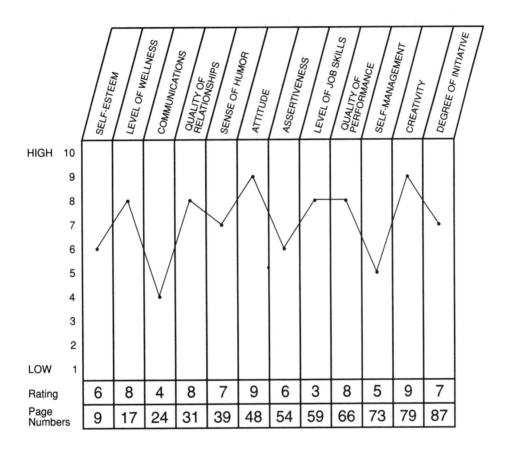

	SELF-ESTEEM	LEVEL OF WELLNESS	COMMUNICATIONS	QUALITY OF RELATIONSHIPS	SENSE OF HUMOR	ATTITUDE	ASSERTIVENESS	LEVEL OF JOB SKILLS	QUALITY OF PERFORMANCE	SELF-MANAGEMENT	CREATIVITY	DEGREE OF INITIATIVE
Rating	6	8	4	8	7	9	6	3	8	5	9	7
Page Numbers	9	17	24	31	39	48	54	59	66	73	79	87

HIGH 10 ... LOW 1

INTERPRETATION:

- When a profile shows only one category below the 5 level, it is a safe bet that concentration to improve that area will pay Beverly substantial and immediate dividends.

- A study of Beverly's profile indicates that improvement in the communications category would improve all of the remaining areas, especially self-esteem and assertiveness. If Beverly were to save the profile while she took a course in communications or public speaking, a second profile should show a measurable change for the better.

- A 1- or 2-point improvement in the self-esteem, self-management and assertiveness categories could contribute significantly to Beverly's career progress.

SAMPLE
INVENTORY PROFILE SHEET
"PAT"

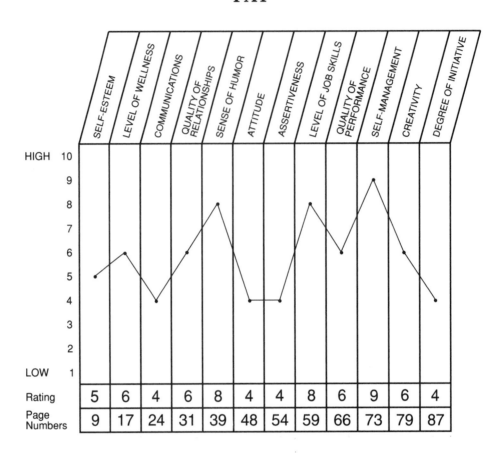

	SELF-ESTEEM	LEVEL OF WELLNESS	COMMUNICATIONS	QUALITY OF RELATIONSHIPS	SENSE OF HUMOR	ATTITUDE	ASSERTIVENESS	LEVEL OF JOB SKILLS	QUALITY OF PERFORMANCE	SELF-MANAGEMENT	CREATIVITY	DEGREE OF INITIATIVE
Rating	5	6	4	6	8	4	4	8	6	9	6	4
Page Numbers	9	17	24	31	39	48	54	59	66	73	79	87

INTERPRETATION:

- With two categories rated 8 or above and all others rated 6 or below (somewhat the reverse of most profiles) this may indicate Pat was too hard in rating herself or is lacking in personal confidence.

- A high rating in humor with low ratings in communications, attitude, and assertiveness might be a signal that Pat enjoys a good sense of humor but does not share it with others.

- The 4 rating in initiative might indicate that Pat sometimes keeps busy with trivial matters while avoiding major challenges.

- The author suggests that Pat could show major improvements by concentrating on the four areas of low ratings (one area per week for four weeks) and then do a second profile for matching purposes.

P A R T

III

Interpreting
Your Profile

TIPS TO FOLLOW

What can you learn from your profile that will improve your personal life and career? Many insightful discoveries are possible, providing you are open and honest with yourself and follow these tips:

Tip #1: Accept the fact that your profile is yours and yours *alone*. It reflects your personality, characteristics, strengths, and weaknesses. It is not a scientific analysis, but puts you into a more favorable position to sense where you can make improvements. The more you study your profile, the more you will gain from it.

Tip #2: Often it is beneficial for you to compare your profile with others. Or to show and discuss your profile with another person you respect who can assist you in making your most valuable interpretation. To help you in making a comparison, an additional profile is provided on pages 106 and 107. You may copy this profile for the use of others. Match any responses with your profile to see if there are any insights you can gain. *Pay particular attention to the author's suggestions (interpretations) at the bottom of each profile.*

Tip #3: Keep in mind that there is no such thing as a perfect or ''model'' profile. Among the twelve categories, we all have our weak areas. Most people who are honest with themselves have at least one column in their profile under 5. If none show up, it may be an indication that the individual is ''blind'' to a weakness that is obvious to others.

Tip #4: A balance between weak and strong areas is often noticeable. For example, an individual may show a 9 or 10 in three areas and a 4 or under in a like number of areas. This is a healthy sign because the very fact that the individual has exceptionally strong areas indicates that the weak areas discovered can be raised. The number one benefit of doing a profile is to discover a weak area where immediate improvement can be made. It is possible for a person to have 7 or 8 very high categories only to have one or two extremely weak areas that are holding the person back from making the career progress that otherwise would occur.

Tip #5: A single area with a score under 5 can have a negative influence on the remaining 11 areas. Example: A low score in INITIATIVE (being a procrastinator) could delay or neutralize the positive effects of other areas. All 12 categories are inter-dependent which means that one very weak area can ''pull down'' one's effectiveness in all other areas.

(continued, overleaf)

TIPS TO FOLLOW (Continued)

Tip #6: By the same token, a very high rating on one or more categories could "pull up" the effectiveness of the individual in other areas. Example: A person who rates high in ATTITUDE and SENSE OF HUMOR probably does better in the COMMUNICATION category than would otherwise be the case.

Tip #7: One should keep in mind that a high score in one area does not necessarily "cover up" the weakness in another area. Example: Lack of job competencies (SKILL CATEGORY) will eventually surface even if the individual has a great ATTITUDE and SENSE OF HUMOR.

Tip #8: Share results selectively with others—especially superiors and career guidance professionals—so that additional insights may be gained.

Tip #9: Build a new profile every few months. If you use a personal computer, put your first profile into storage and add new ones for comparison purposes. This will help you track your progress.

Tip #10: Loan your book and inventory to co-workers and friends to help them when they are going through "down periods." Or present them with a book of their own.

Tip #11: Build your own self-help library. More and more ambitious career people are turning to self-help programs to maintain their motivation. You can start your library by selecting from the titles shown on page 101, or order others listed in the back of this book.

Tip #12: When necessary, see a professional. As far as most categories are concerned, improvement remains a do-it-yourself challenge. This does not imply, however, that professional assistance should be avoided. Just the opposite. When the battery in your car runs down, a recharge is the first possibility. But sometimes a new generator, cable, or battery is the solution. When personal problems are critical, seeing a professional counselor and possibly joining a support group can be a wise choice. This is especially true in the field of mental health.

IMPROVING NEGLECTED AREAS

A single FIFTY MINUTE self-help book is referenced for each of the twelve profile categories below. Although other books in or out of the FIFTY-MINUTE SERIES may support an area, only the one with the closest identification has been selected. Please check your weak categories and consider ordering a book to start your personal improvement program.

PROFILE CATEGORY	FIFTY MINUTE BOOK
SELF-ESTEEM ☐	*Developing Self Esteem: A Positive Guide To Personal Success* Author: Connie Palladino, Ph.D.
WELLNESS ☐	*Personal Wellness* Author: Rich Griggs
COMMUNICATION ☐	*The Art of Communicating* Author: Bert Decker, President, Decker Communications
HUMAN SKILLS ☐	*Winning At Human Relations* Author: Elwood N. Chapman
HUMOR ☐	*Making Humor Work* Author: Terry Paulson, Ph.D.
ATTITUDE ☐	*Attitude: Your Most Priceless Possession* Author: Elwood N. Chapman
ASSERTIVENESS ☐	*Developing Positive Assertiveness* Author: Sam R. Lloyd, President, Success Systems, Inc.
SKILLS ☐	*The College Experience* Author: Elwood N. Chapman
QUALITY ☐	*Quality At Work* Author: Diane Bone & Rick Griggs
SELF-MANAGEMENT ☐	*Successful Self-Management* Author: Paul M. Timm, Ph.D.
CREATIVITY ☐	*Creativity In Business* Author: Carol Gorman, Ph.D.
INITIATIVE ☐	*Stop Procrastinating: Get To Work!* Author: James Sherman

Twelve Steps to Self-Improvement

DEVOTE A WEEK TO IMPROVE EACH OF YOUR WEAK AREAS

A weak area is one that is 4 or more points below your strongest category. It is one where improvement is indicated and where results can be achieved and noticed by management. A primary purpose of the profile you have completed is to discover your weak areas.

Experience shows that for most people:

- Trying to improve in too many areas at the same time results in confusion and lack of motivation to continue.

- Concentrating on a single area (humor, assertiveness, etc.) for a period of one week produces the best results.

If the week-at-a-time idea fits into your way of thinking, you may wish to complete the chart below and post it where it can act as a reminder. Start with your weakest area and continue until you have brought all categories that are weak to a more satisfactory level.

WEEKLY SELF-IMPROVEMENT SCHEDULE

Week #1: _____
(category)

Week #2: _____
(category)

Week #3: _____
(category)

Week #4: _____
(category)

SUGGESTED ANSWERS TO CASES

ANSWER CASE #1 (Jill): One possibility would be to sit down with Jill for at least an hour, and together work out a list of "action steps" that could help her push her self-esteem higher. Such steps could include: (1) helping Jill improve her physical image through an "investment" in grooming; (2) assisting her in having and keeping more social contacts; (3) getting her to "open up" and talk more to others on a wide variety of subjects. (One good way to do this is teach her the art of asking questions.); (4) having Jill talk with her supervisor about steps she could take to make her more promotable; (5) giving Jill as many compliments as possible to help her build a higher self-esteem; (6) recommending she take a course in public speaking.

ANSWER CASE #2 (James): It would appear that James is afraid to move out of the protective shell he has built around himself. He needs to mix with others on a more open basis so he will receive the compliments he deserves. Joining a health club or engaging in some other non-work activity with co-workers might help. As a friend, you need to actually get him started in some fun activities where he can mix with others.

ANSWER CASE #3 (Genelle): She may need help in understanding that gaining and losing weight regularly is detrimental to her overall wellness. Consistency in exercise and diet seems to evade Genelle. Perhaps the next time she comes close to a recommended weight, she can learn to keep from getting so excited over her new image that she forgets her weight program. Genelle is paying a very high price for her lack of discipline. Also suggest that she talk it over with her doctor.

ANSWER CASE #4 (Karl): Depending upon the quality and strength of the relationship between them, Maggie might consider one or all of the following: (1) Read a good book on wellness and discuss appropriate passages with Karl. (2) Ask Karl if she can accompany him when he takes his physical examination so the subject can be discussed with a professional. (3) Introduce for discussion the impact his exhaustion is having on his career, family relationships, and his long-term goals.

ANSWER CASE #5 (Charlie): Although the supervisor should assume a good share of the responsibility, a major portion may belong to Charlie because he failed to keep communication lines open and let his emotional feelings dissipate. In short, Charlie allowed himself to be victimized by refusing to take action to restore the relationship or seeking a new career start elsewhere.

ANSWER CASE #6 (Melissa): The supervisor needs to get through to Melissa that employees who are basically silent are always misunderstood. Open communication is required to be a good team member. Some "small talk" and laughter is necessary for most members to produce at an acceptable "team" level. Perhaps the supervisor could make a practice of including Melissa more during internal sessions to give her the opportunity to "open up" so others can get to know and support her.

ANSWER CASE #7 (Courtney): All working environments seem to have a few negative people. In Courtney's case, the situation appears more severe. Even so, she should be able to throw up a shield of positive thoughts so that she is not pulled down to their negative level. Perhaps she, the other positive employees, and the supervisor can devise and carry out a strategy to improve things. Most people learn to get along with negative co-workers or family members without it having a serious impact upon their mental health.

ANSWER CASE #8 (Trisha): Yes, even when other candidates can be better in other areas, a sense of humor can make the final difference. Laughter created by a supervisor can bring a team closer together, strengthen other characteristics within the individual (especially attitude), and is a measure of good mental health. In general, a happy, relaxed departmental staff produces more and greater productivity and is the reason why Trish was selected.

ANSWER CASE #9 (Shannon): There is no evidence other than observation that this is possible. However, it seems logical that a negative view in one major part of life has a ''pull down'' or ''draining'' effect on another part. By the same token, a positive view in two or more environments can be mutually supportive and the individual could become even more positive in all other areas.

ANSWER CASE #10 (Kim): If Alice does anything to help Kim it should be a very slow process so that Kim does not lose her natural charm and effectiveness. In short, she should learn to assert herself slowly and in her own way. Kim could invite Alice to attend a seminar on assertive behavior with her. They could then spend time analyzing the behavior of others who are non-assertive, assertive, and aggressive so that Kim might see herself in a role where she would be most effective. Slowly, as she builds more confidence and understands Western ways, Kim will find her own ''comfort zone'' as far as assertiveness is concerned.

ANSWER CASE #11 (Joanne): It sounds like Joanne had so much success when she first started being more assertive that it went to her head and she over-stepped her natural limits. When the ill feelings she is creating eventually come back to Joanne in full force, it is possible she will reevaluate what has happened to her and learn to take a softer and more effective approach. In the meantime, her superior should initiate a series of counseling sessions to discuss the differences between assertive and aggressive behavior and tell her directly the affect her behavior is having on her co-workers.

ANSWER CASE #12 (Felicia): No. Felicia is forgetting that as a supervisor, she will have the responsibility of training those in her department. This means she needs to know *more* about new computer hardware and software, not less. She will, however, be able to train one member of the team to train others so she can have more time for supervisory duties in the field of human relations and management. With a little more concentration on keeping her computer skills at a high level, Felicia might make an excellent supervisor.

ANSWER CASE #13 (Victor): If you feel that you are a mentor for Victor, Strategy 3 might be best and most convincing. This will have the added advantage of slowing him down a little in favor of quality to improve his relationship with you. The discussion might be best over lunch where there is less pressure and Victor can express why he is in such a hurry to reach his goals.

ANSWER CASE #14 (Rica and Rolph): The author prefers Rolph's plan because of the good feeling that occurs when one leaves an organized plan behind. For many, this approach enables people to relax more and dissipate normal stress. Either plan, however, can be effective.

ANSWER CASE #15 (Darlene): Darlene is missing the point. If she would apply the same techniques at home that she uses at work she would have even more free time and a happier lifestyle. For example, she would save time and money in the long run and improve the quality of her free time. Anyone as organized as Darlene in the work environment should have plenty of energy left to have a more organized homelife that would set her free to find greater personal fulfillment.

ANSWER CASE #16 (Jerry): Jerry may be jumping the gun for two reasons. First, Ms. North may actually be waiting for a winning idea. Second, Jerry may be over-estimating his creative suggestions. In addition, it may be dangerous for Jerry to go over Ms. North's head without a two-way discussion in advance. Of course, if her boss reacts in a humorous way to Jerry's written presentation, it could bring the attention he seeks. He should realize, of course, that his strategy carries a risk.

ANSWER CASE #17 (Jess): It is doubtful. In all probability, the system would be just another idea that Jess would consider but never fulfill. Perhaps his problem is having a goal (marriage to a certain person, new home at a favorable location, or to prove to a peer that he is is more capable than the person thought) rather than a system. Most people need an emotional goal to make improvements—not just a system that will make it easier.

SUPPLEMENTAL PROFILE SHEET

	SELF-ESTEEM	LEVEL OF WELLNESS	COMMUNICATIONS	QUALITY OF RELATIONSHIPS	SENSE OF HUMOR	ATTITUDE
HIGH 10						
9						
8						
7						
6						
5						
4						
3						
2						
LOW 1						
Rating						
Page Numbers	9	17	24	31	39	48

ASSERTIVENESS	LEVEL OF JOB SKILLS	QUALITY OF PERFORMANCE	SELF-MANAGEMENT	CREATIVITY	DEGREE OF INITIATIVE	
						10 HIGH
						9
						8
						7
						6
						5
						4
						3
						2
						1 LOW
						Rating
54	59	66	73	79	87	Page Numbers

NOTES

NOTES

NOTES

NOTES

OVER 150 BOOKS AND 35 VIDEOS AVAILABLE IN THE 50-MINUTE SERIES

We hope you enjoyed this book. If so, we have good news for you. This title is part of the best-selling *50-MINUTE*™ *Series* of books. All *Series* books are similar in size and identical in price. Many are supported with training videos.

To order *50-MINUTE* Books and Videos or request a free catalog, contact your local distributor or Crisp Publications, Inc., 1200 Hamilton Court, Menlo Park, CA 94025. Our toll-free number is (800) 442-7477.

50-Minute Series Books and Videos Subject Areas . . .

Management
Training
Human Resources
Customer Service and Sales Training
Communications
Small Business and Financial Planning
Creativity
Personal Development
Wellness
Adult Literacy and Learning
Career, Retirement and Life Planning

Other titles available from Crisp Publications in these categories

Crisp Computer Series
The Crisp Small Business & Entrepreneurship Series
Quick Read Series
Management
Personal Development
Retirement Planning